AA

SPANISH

DISCARDS

About this book

Jane Wightwick
had the idea

Wina Gunn
wrote the pages

Leila & Zeinah Gaafar
(aged 10 and 12) drew the
first pictures in
each chapter

Robert Bowers
(aged 52) drew the other
pictures, and designed
the book

Ana Bremon
did the Spanish stuff

Important things that
must be included

© **g-and-w publishing** 2013

All rights reserved. This publication or any part of it may not
be copied or reproduced by any means without the prior
permission of the publisher. All enquiries should be directed
to the publisher.

A CIP catalogue record for this book is available from the
British Library

ISBN: 978-07495-7419-2

Published by **AA Publishing** (a trading name of AA Media
Limited, whose registered office is Fanum House, Basing
View, Basingstoke, Hampshire RG21 4EA. Registered number
06112600)

Printed and bound in China by 1010 Printing International Ltd

Cover design by Nick Johnston

A04959

What's inside

Making friends

How to be cool with the group

Wanna play?

Our guide to joining in everything from hide-and-seek to the latest electronic game

Feeling hungry

Order your favourite foods or go local

Looking good

Make sure you keep up with all those essential fashions

Hanging out

At the pool, beach, or theme park – don't miss out on the action

70

Pocket money

Spend it here!

90

Grown-up talk

blah!
blah!
blah!
blah!

If you really, really have to!

100

Extra stuff

All the handy things – numbers, months, time, days of the week

108

MAKING FRIENDS

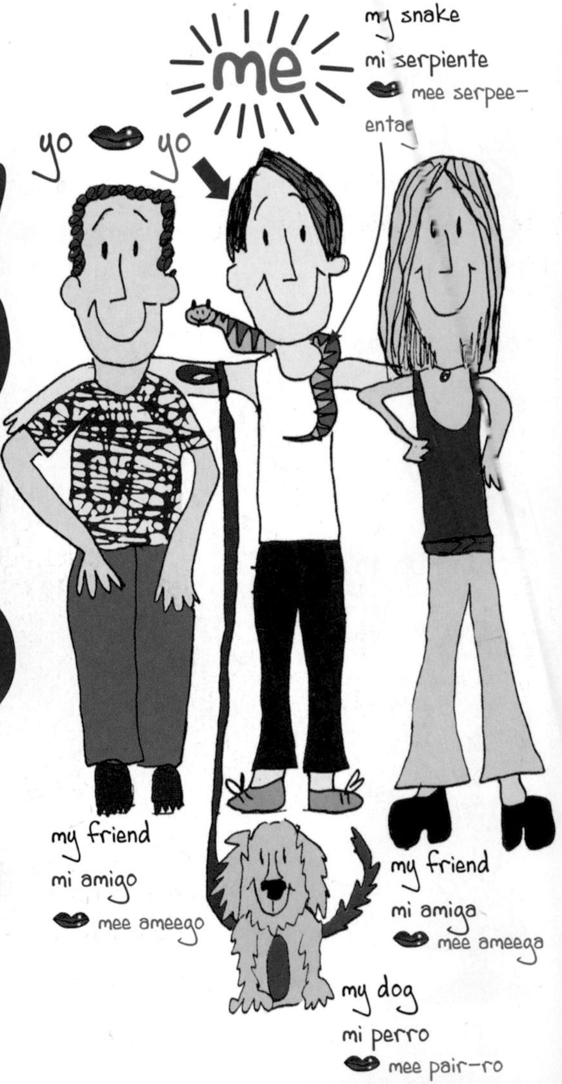

my big brother
mi hermano mayor
💋 mee airmano my-yor

grandpa
abuelo
💋 abwelo

grandma
abuela
💋 abwela

dad
papá
💋 pa-pah

mum mamá
💋 ma-mah

my little sister
mi hermana pequeña
💋 mee airmana

pekenya

MAKING FRIENDS

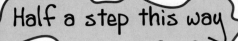

Half a step this way

stepfather/stepmother
padrastro/madrastra
🗣 padrastro/madrastra

stepbrother/stepsister
hermanastro/hermanastra
🗣 airmanastro/airmanastra

half brother/half sister
medio hermano/medio hermana
🗣 medyo airmano/
medyo airmana

Hi!
¡Hola!
🗣 ola

What's your name?
¿Cómo te llamas?
🗣 komo tay yamas

My name's ...
Me llamo ...
🗣 may yamo

The Spanish put an upside-down question mark before a question, as well as one the right way up at the end. It's the same with exclamation marks.

¿Isn't that weird?   ¡You bet!

Are you OK?
¿Estás bien?
👄 estas beeyen

Cool, and you?
Guay, ¿y tú?
👄 gwhy. ee too

Where are you from?
¿De dónde eres?
👄 day donday air-res

from Canada

de Canadá

 day canadah

from Ireland

de Irlanda

 day eerlanda

from Scotland

de Escocia

 day escothya

from Wales del País de Gales

 del pie-yis day gal-les

That means "the land of the Gauls".

from the United States

de los Estados Unidos

day los estados ooneedos

from England

de Inglaterra

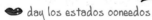 day eengla-tairra

10

Los SMS

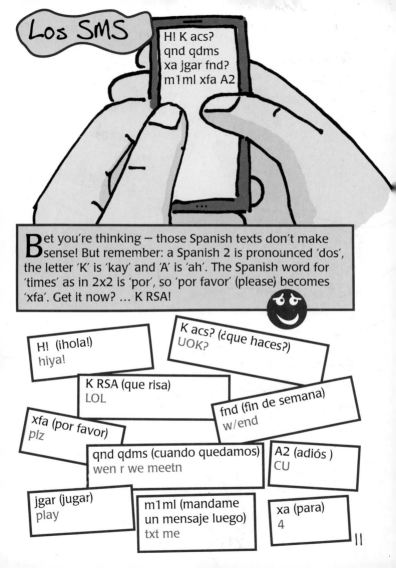

H! K acs?
qnd qdms
xa jgar fnd?
m1ml xfa A2

Bet you're thinking – those Spanish texts don't make sense! But remember: a Spanish 2 is pronounced 'dos', the letter 'K' is 'kay' and 'A' is 'ah'. The Spanish word for 'times' as in 2x2 is 'por', so 'por favor' (please) becomes 'xfa'. Get it now? … K RSA!

H! (¡hola!)
hiya!

K acs? (¿que haces?)
UOK?

K RSA (que risa)
LOL

fnd (fin de semana)
w/end

xfa (por favor)
plz

qnd qdms (cuando quedamos)
wen r we meetn

A2 (adiós)
CU

jgar (jugar)
play

m1ml (mandame
un mensaje luego)
txt me

xa (para)
4

11

How old are you?

¿Cuántos años tienes?

🗣 kwantos anyos tee-enes

12 years old

Doce años

🗣 dothay anyos

Happy birthday!

¡Cumpleaños feliz!

🗣 koomplay-anyos faileeth

What's your star sign?

¿Qué signo del zodiaco eres?

🗣 kay signo del thodee-ako air-res

When's your birthday?

¿Cuándo es tu cumpleaños?

🗣 kwando es too koomplay-anyos

12

Star signs

AQUARIUS

Jan. 21 – Feb. 19
Acuario 💋 akwaree-o

PISCES

Feb. 20 – Mar. 20
Piscis 💋 pees-thees

ARIES
Mar. 21 – Apr. 20
Aries 💋 a-rees

TAURUS

Apr. 21 – May. 21
Tauro 💋 towro

GEMINI

May 22 – June 21
Géminis 💋 hemeenees

CANCER

June 22 – July 23
Cáncer 💋 kanthair

LEO
July 24 – Aug. 23
Leo 💋 leo

VIRGO

Aug. 24 – Sep. 23
Virgo 💋 beergo

LIBRA

Sep. 24 – Oct. 23
Libra 💋 leebra

SCORPIO

Oct. 24 – Nov. 22
Escorpio 💋 eskorpee-o

SAGITTARIUS
Nov. 23 – Dec. 21
Sagitario 💋 sa-heetaree-o

CAPRICORN

Dec. 22 – Jan. 20
Capricornio 💋 kapreecornee-o

football el fútbol
🗣 el footbol

rollerblading
el patinaje en línea
🗣 el patee–nahay
en leenya

music
la música
🗣 la mooseeka

electronic games
los juegos electrónicos
🗣 los hway–gos elektroneekos

tv
la tele
🗣 la taylay

comics
los tebeos
🗣 los taybayos

spiders las arañas
🗣 las aranyas

school
el colegio
🗣 el kolay–heeyo

What's your ...?
¿Cuál es tu ...?
👄 kwal es too ...

favourite groop
grupo preferido
👄 groopo prefereedo

favourite colour
color preferido
👄 kol-lor prefereedo

Page 69

favourite game
juego preferido
👄 hway-go prefereedo

favourite food
comida preferida
🗣 komeeda prefereeda

favourite ringtone
tono preferido
🗣 tone-oh prefereedo

favourite animal
animal preferido
🗣 anee-mal prefereedo

favourite team
equipo preferido
🗣 ekeepo prefereedo

Talk about your pets

He's hungry

Está hambriento

💋 esta ambree-yento

She's sleeping

Está durmiendo

💋 esta doormee-yendo

Can I stroke your dog?

¿Puedo acariciar tu perro?

💋 pwedo atharee-thyar
too pair-ro

Do you have
any pets?

¿Tienes alguna
mascota?

💋 tee-enes algoona
mascota

18

dog
el perro
🗣 el pair–ro

cat
el gato
🗣 el gato

snake
la serpiente
🗣 la serpee–entay

guinea pig
la cobaya
🗣 la kob–eye–a

hamster
el hámster
🗣 el hamstair

parakeet
el periquito
🗣 el peree–keeto

My little doggy goes *guau guau!*

A Spanish doggy (that's "guauguau" in baby language) doesn't say "woof, woof", it says *"guau, guau"* (*gwa-oo, gwa-oo*). A Spanish bird says *"pío, pío"* (*pee-o, pee-o*) and "cock-a-doodle-do" in Spanish chicken-speak is *"kikirikí"* (*kee-kee ree-kee*). But a cat does say *"miaow"* and a cow *"moo"* whether they're speaking Spanish or English!

19

Talk about school (if you can stand it)

geography
la geografía
👄 la heogra-feeya

PE
la gimnasia
👄 la heem-naseeya

art
el dibujo artístico
👄 el deebooho arteesteeko

Spanish
m.smith
form 2b

Spanish
el español
👄 el espanyol

maths
las mates
👄 las mat-tes

20

music
la música
🗣 la mooseeka

English
el inglés
🗣 el eeng-les

history
la historia
🗣 la eestoreeya

science
las naturales
🗣 las natoorar-les

21

IT
TI
👄 tay-ee

Way unfair!

Spanish children hardly ever have to wear uniform to school and have very long holidays: 10 weeks in the summer and another 5–6 weeks throughout the rest of the year. But before you turn green with envy, you might not like the mounds of *"deberes para las vacaciones"* (*debair-res para las bakathee-yones*), that's "vacation homework"! And if you fail your exams, the teachers could make you repeat the whole year with your little sister!

Talk about your phone

That's ancient
¡Qué anticuado!
🗨 kay antee-kwado

I've run out of credit
Me he quedado sin saldo
🗨 may ay kay-dado seen saldo

What's your mobile phone like?
¿Cómo es tu móvil?
🗨 komo es too mo-beel

Lucky!
¡Qué suerte!
🗨 kay swair-tay

What a cool ringtone!
¡Qué tono más chulo!
🗨 kay tone-oh mass choolo

23

Gossip

Can you keep a secret?

¿Puedes guardar un secreto?

🗣 pwedes gwardar oon sekreto

Do you have a boyfriend (a girlfriend)?

¿Tienes novio (novia)?

🗣 tee-enes nobyo (nobya)

An OK guy/An OK girl

Un tío majo/Una tía maja

🗣 oon teeyo maho/ oona teeya maha

What a bossy-boots!

¡Qué mandón!

🗣 kay man-don

He/She's nutty!

¡Está como una cabra!

🗣 esta komo oona kabra

That means "He/She's like a goat"!

I'm not like that at all!

What a misery guts!

¡Qué malasombra!

🗣 kay malas-sombra

24

You won't make many friends saying this!

Shut up!
¡Cállate! 👄 kigh-yatay

Bog off!
¡Vete a la porra! 👄 betay a la porra

If you're fed up with someone, and you want to say something like "you silly …!" or "you stupid …!", you can start with **"pedazo de"** (which actually means "piece of …") and add anything you like. What about …

Stupid banana!
¡Pedazo de plátano!
(pedatho day platano)

or …

Silly sausage!
¡Pedazo de salchicha! (pedatho day salcheecha)

Take your pick. It should do the trick. You could also try **"¡pedazo de idiota!"** (pedatho day eedee-ota). You don't need a translation here, do you?

You might have to say

Bother!

¡Ostras!

 os-stras

That means "Oysters"!

"Did someone call us?"

Rats!

¡Porras!

 porras

That's not funny

No tiene gracia

 no tee-eray

gra-theeya

I'm fed up

¡Estoy harto! (boys)

¡Estoy harta! (girls)

 estoy arto/estoy arta

That's plenty!

¡Ya vale!

 ya balay

Stop!

¡No hagas eso!

🗨 no agas eso

I want to go home!

¡Me quiero ir a casa!

🗨 may kyairo eer ah kassa

I don't care

Me da igual

🗨 may da eegwal

At last!

¡Por fin!

🗨 por feen

Saying goodbye

Here's my address
Aquí tienes mi dirección
👄 akee tee-enes mee
deerek-thyon

What's your address?
¿Cuál es tu dirección?
👄 kwal es too deerek-thyon

Come to visit me
Ven a visitarme
👄 ben a beesee-tarmay

Have a good trip!

¡Buen viaje!

 bwen bee-ahay

Write to me soon

Escríbeme pronto

 eskree-bemay pronto

Send me a text

Envíame un SMS

 envee-armay oon "SMS"

Let's chat online

¿Chateamos?

 chatay-amos

Bye!

¡Adiós

 adeeyos

What's your email address?

¿Cuál es tu mail?

 kwal es too mail

WANNA PLAY?

el elástico
🗣 el elasteeko

el ping-pong
🗣 el "ping-pong"

MP3 player
el reproductor
👄 el raypro-
dooktor

el móvil
👄 el mo-beel

el yo-yó
👄 el "yo yo"

Do you want to play ...?

¿Quieres jugar ....?

💋 keyair-res hoogar

... table football?

... al futbolín?

💋 al footboleen

... cards?

... a las cartas?

💋 a las kartas

... on the computer?

... con el ordenador?

💋 kon el orden-ador

... noughts and crosses?

... a las tres en raya?

💋 a las trays en righ-ya

... hide and seek?
... al escondite?
👄 al eskon-deetay

... catch?
... al balón?
👄 al ballon

Not now
Ahora no
👄 a-ora no

Yeah!
¡Vale!
👄 balay

Fancy a game of **foal** or **donkey**?!

In Spain, you don't play "leap frog", you play "foal" – *el potro*. There is also a group version of this called "donkey" – *el burro*. This involves two teams. Team 1 line up in a row with their heads down in the shape of a donkey. Team 2 take it in turns to leap as far as they can onto the back of the "donkey". If the donkey falls over, Team 2 win. If Team 2 touch the ground or can't leap far enough to get all the team on, then Team 1 win – got that?! Spanish children will try to tell you this is enormous fun, but your parents might not be so keen on the bruises!

Can my friend play too?

¿Mi amigo también puede jugar?

mee ameego tam–byen

pway–day hoogar

I have to ask my parents

Se lo tengo que pedir a mis padres

say loe tengo kay pedeer

ah mees padrays

Make yourself heard

Who dares?

You're it!

¡La quedas tú!

👄 la kedas too

Race you!

¿Una carrera?

👄 oona karraire

I'm first

Soy el primero (boys)

Soy la primera (girls)

👄 soy el preemairo

soy la preemaira

Electronic games

la pantalla
💋 la pan-tie-ya

el CD-Rom
💋 el thay-day rom

el ratón
💋 el rat-ton

HIGH SCORES
Frank
Robert
Leila
Sarah
Jean-Paul
Denis
Nina
Jane

el ratón
💋 el rat-ton

el teclado
💋 el teklado

el micro
💋 el meek-ro

los cascos
💋 los kas-kos

38

Show me

Enséñame

 ensay–nyamay

What do I do?

¿Qué hay que hacer?

 kay eye kay athair

Am I dead?

¿Me han matado?

may an matado

Shoot–em–up!

¡Dispárales!

deespar–ralayz

How many lives do I have?

¿Cuántas vidas tengo?

kwantas beedas tengo

How many levels are there?

¿Cuántos niveles hay?

kwantos neebay–les eye

39

It's virtual fun!

Do you have WiFi?

¿Tienes wifi?

💋 teeyenes weefee

Make sure you say it like this to avoid blank looks!

Send me a message.
Mándame un mensaje.

How do i join?
¿Cómo me apunto?

I'm not old enough.
No tengo edad suficiente.

I'm not allowed.
No tengo permiso.

I don't know who you are.
No te conozco.

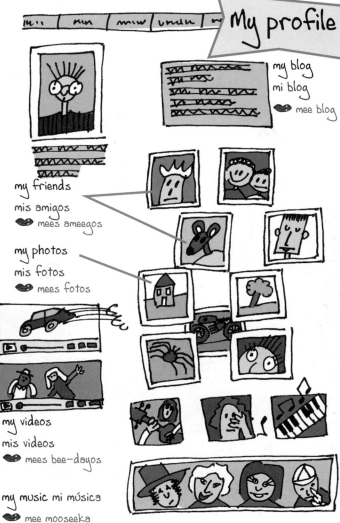

my blog
mi blog
mee blog

my friends
mis amigos
mees ameegos

my photos
mis fotos
mees fotos

my videos
mis videos
mees bee-dayos

my music mi música
mee mooseeka

Non couch-potato activities!

tennis
el tenis
🗣 el tenees

trampolining
el trampolín
🗣 el "trampoline"

bowling
los bolos
🗣 los bol-les

swimming
la natación
🗣 la nata-thyon

42

hockey

el hockey

💋 el "hockey"

gymnastics

la gimnasia

💋 la heem-nasya

ballet

el ballet

💋 el ballay

basketball

el baloncesto

💋 el ballon-thesto

and, of course, we haven't forgotten *"el fútbol"*... (P.T.O.) 43

f⚽️tball

boots

las botas

🗣 las botas

football kit

el equipo de fútbol

🗣 el ekeepo day footbol

ref

el árbitro

🗣 el arbeetro

shin pads

las espinilleras

🗣 las espinee-yeras

Good save!

¡Vaya parada!

🗣 baya parada

Pass! ¡Pasa!

🗣 pasa

44

Keeping the others in line

Not like that!
¡Así no!
👄 asee no

You cheat! ¡Tramposo! (boys only)
¡Tramposa! (girls only)
👄 tramposo/tramposa

I'm not playing
anymore
Ya no juego
👄 ya no hwego

It's not fair!
¡No es justo!
👄 no es hoosto

Stop it!
¡No hagas eso!
👄 no agas eso

Showing off

... do a handstand?

... hacer el pino?

🗣 athair el peeno

Can you ...

¿Sabes ...

🗣 sabays

Look at me!

¡Mírame!

🗣 meera-may

... do a cartwheel?

... dar volteretas laterales?

🗣 dar boltair-retas latairal-les

... do this?

... hacer esto?

🗣 athair esto

48

Impress your Spanish friends with this!

You can show off to your new Spanish friends by practising this tongue twister:

Tres tristes tigres comían trigo en un trigal.

trays treestays teegrays comee-an treego en oon treegal

(This means "Three sad tigers ate wheat in a wheat field".)

Then see if they can do as well with this English one:

"She sells seashells on the seashore, but the shells she sells aren't seashells, I'm sure."

For a rainy day

pack of cards
una baraja de cartas
 oona baraha day kartas

my deal/your deal
yo doy/tú das
yo doy/too das

king
el rey
el ray

queen
la reina
la ray-eena

jack
la jota
la hota

joker
el komodín
el komodeen

tréboles
trebol-les

corazones
korazon-nes

picas
peekas

diamantes
dee-amantays

Do you have the ace of swords?!

You might also see Spanish children playing with a different pack of cards. There are only 48 cards instead of 52 and the suits are also different. Instead of clubs, spades, diamonds and hearts, there are gold coins (**oros**), swords (**espadas**), cups (**copas**) and batons (**bastos**).

chessboard el tablero

🗨 el tablairo

bishop el alfil

🗨 el alfeel

knight el caballo

🗨 el kab-eye-o

pawn el peón

🗨 el pay-on

king el rey

🗨 el ray

rook
la torre

🗨 la torray

queen la reina

🗨 la ray-eena

FEELING HUNGRY

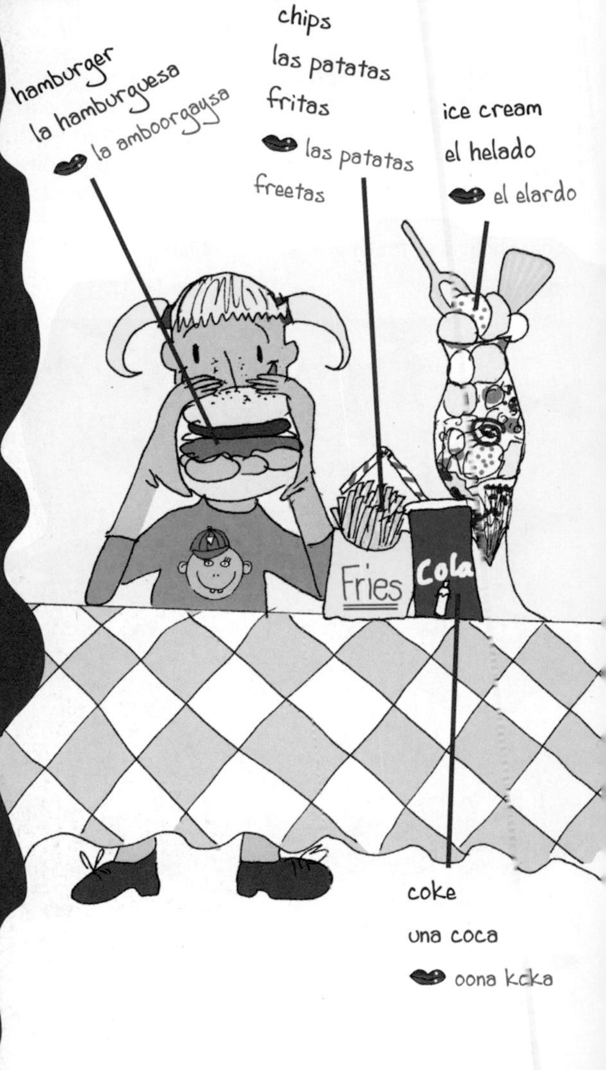

creme caramel

el flan

👄 el flan

(Watch out! "Flan" in Spanish doesn't mean a pastry tart with cheese!)

squid

los calamares

👄 los kalamar-res

la paella

👄 la pie-eyya

orange juice

el zumo de naranja

👄 el thoomo day

naran-ha

FEELING HUNGRY

Grub

I'm starving

Tengo un hambre de lobo

💋 tengo oon ambray day lobo

el lobo

That means "I have the hunger of a wolf"!

Please can I have ...

Por favor, me da ...

💋 por fabor, may da

... a croissant

un cruasán

 oon krwasan

... a cream bun

un bollo con nata

 oon boyo kon nata

... a puff pastry

una palmera

 oona palmayra

... a waffle

un gofre

oon go-fray

... a muffin

una magdalena

 oona magda-layna

los churros

 los choorros

These are wonderful sugary doughnut-like snacks. They are sold in cafés and kiosks and usually come in a paper cone. They are also very popular for breakfast in winter, with thick hot chocolate (***chocolate con churros***).

You: Can I have some churros, Mum?

Mum: No. They'll make you fat and rot your teeth.

You: But I think it's good to experience a foreign culture through authentic local food.

Mum: Oh, all right then.

Churros? *"¡Mm, mm!"*, Garlic sandwich? *"¡Agh!"*. If you're going to make foody noises you'll need to know how to do it properly in Spanish!

"Yum, yum!" is out in Spanish. You should say *"¡Mm, mm!"*. And "Yuk!" is *"¡Agh!"* (pronounced *"ag"*), but be careful not to let adults hear you say this!

Drink up

I'm dying for a drink
Me muero de sed
👄 may mwero day sed

I'd like ...
Me apetece ...
👄 may apay-taythay

... a coke
... una coca
👄 oona koka

... an orange juice
... un zumo de naranja
👄 oon thoomo day naran-ha

... an apple juice
... un zumo de manzana
👄 oon thoomo day manthana

... a lemonade
una Fanta® de limón

😛 oona Fanta
day leemon

In Spain ask for
**una Fanta® de
limón** when you
want a lemonade
or **Fanta® de naranja** (*fanta
day naran-ha*) for a fizzy
orange. Fanta® is the most
popular type and so that's
what people say.

... water agua

😛 agwa

... a milkshake
... un batido

😛 oon bateedo

You get your hot
chocolate in a large cup
(to dunk your churros in).

... a hot chocolate
... un chocolate

😛 oon chokolatay

58

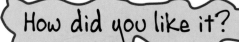

How did you like it?

That's lovely

Eso está super bueno

 eso esta

soopair bweno

That's gorgeous

Eso está delicioso

 eso esta daylee—

thee—oso

I don't like that

Eso no me gusta

 eso no may goosta

I'm stuffed

Voy a explotar

boy a explotar

I can't eat that

No me lo puedo comer

 no may lo pwedo komair

That's gross

Está asqueroso

 esta askairoso

Tap into *Tapas*

There's a perfect way to try a little bit of everything in Spain and that's "*tapas*". These are little snacks that everyone eats in cafés and bars (which the adults might insist on going to). *Tapas* come in little dishes and are a great way of finding out if you like something without risking a torrent of abuse if you leave an expensive meal untouched.

Here are four of the most popular:

tortilla

🫘 tortee-ya

Spanish omelette – thick and comes in slices

croquetas

🫘 kroketas

egg-shaped rissoles filled with chicken, ham or fish

albóndigas

🫘 albon-deegas

meatballs in tomato sauce

calamares a la romana

🫘 kalamar-res a la romana

squid rings

60

Parties

balloon el globo
🗨 el glow-bo

Can I have
some more?
¿Puedo tener un
poco más?
🗨 pwaydo tenair
oon poko mas

party hat
el gorro de fiesta
🗨 el gorro day fee-esta

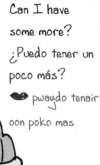

This is for you
Esto es para ti
🗨 esto es para tee

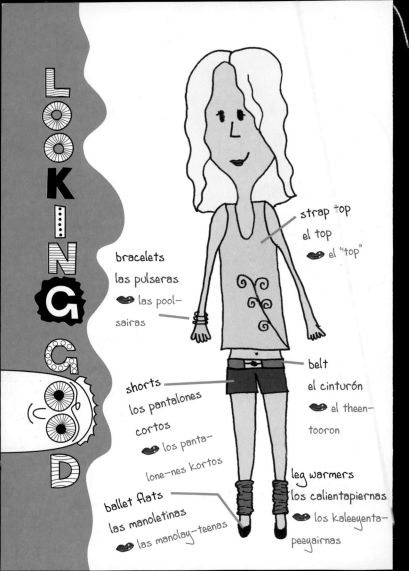

cap
la gorra
🗣 la gorra

earphones
los auriculares
🗣 los owree-
koolar-res

hoodie
la capucha
🗣 la kapoocha

jeans
los vaqueros
🗣 los bakayros

trainers
ortivas
r-teebas

LOOKING GOOD

Clothes

jeans
los vaqueros
👄 los bakayros

sweatshirt
la sudadera
👄 la sooda-
dayra

T-shirt
la camiseta
👄 la kameeseta

football shirt
la camiseta de fútbol
👄 la kameeseta day footbol

trainers
las deportivas
👄 las daypor-teebas

shoes
los zapatos
👄 los thapa

skirt
la falda
🗣 la falda

dress
el traje
🗣 el trahay

trousers
los pantalones
🗣 los panta-lone-nes

A pair of cowboys?

The word for jeans in Spanish (**los vaqueros** – *los bakayros*) actually means "cowboys" because they were the first people to wear these trousers.

65

That T-shirt, please
Esa camiseta, por favor
🗨 esa kameeseta, por fabor

Cool tattoo!
¡Qué calcamonía más chula!
🗨 kay kalka-mcneeya mass choola

The pink frilly one
La rosa con volantitos
🗨 la rosa kon bolantaetos

Awesome miniskirt!
¡Vaya minifalda mas chula!
🗨 baya meenee falda mass choola

The purple stripey one
La morada de rayas
🗨 la morada day righ-yas

spotty
de lunares
🗣 day loonar-res

flowery
de flores
🗣 day flor-res

frilly
con volantitos
🗣 kon bolanteetos

glittery
con brillos
🗣 kon breeyos

stripey
de rayas
🗣 day righ-yas

67

Make it up!

lip gloss
el brillo de labios

👄 el breeyo day labyos

glitter gel
la brillantina

👄 la breeyan-teena

I need a mirror
Necesito un espejo

👄 netthayseeto oon espay-ho

nail varnish
el pintauñas

👄 el peentaw-nyas

earrings los pendientes

👄 los pend-yentays

eye shadow
la sombra de ojos

👄 la sombray day o-hos

Can I borrow your straighteners?
¿Me dejas tu alisador de pelo?

👄 may day-has too alee-sadoor day pay-lo

68

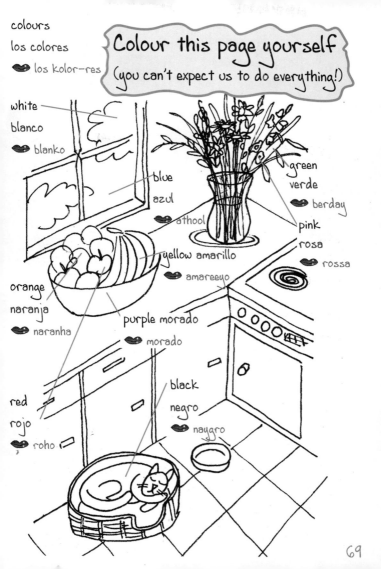

colours

los colores

👄 los kolor-res

Colour this page yourself (you can't expect us to do everything!)

white

blanco

👄 blanko

blue

azul

👄 athool

green

verde

👄 berday

pink

rosa

👄 rossa

yellow amarillo

👄 amareeyo

orange

naranja

👄 naranha

purple morado

👄 morado

red

rojo

👄 roho

black

negro

👄 naygro

What should we do?

¿Qué hacemos?

👄 kay athay-mos

Can I come?

¿Puedo ir?

👄 pwedo eer

Where do you all hang out?

¿Por dónde salís vosotros?

👄 por donday salees bos-otros

That's really wicked

Eso es chachi

👄 eso es chachee

I'm (not) allowed

(No) me dejan

👄 (no) may day-han

Let's go back Regresemos

💋 regray—saymos

That gives me goose bumps (or "chicken flesh" in Spanish!)

Eso me pone la carne de gallina

💋 eso may ponay la karnay day gayeena

I'm bored to death

Me muero de aburrimiento

💋 may mwero day aburree—mee—ento

That's a laugh

Te ríes cantidad

💋 tay reeyes kanteedad

73

Beach babes

Can I borrow this?

¿Me dejas esto?

💋 may dehas esto

Let's hit the beach

Vamos a la playa

💋 bamos a la playa

Is this your bucket?

¿Es tuyo este cubo?

💋 es tooyo estay koobo

You can bury me

Me puedes enterrar

💋 pay pwedes entair-rar

Stop throwing sand!

¡Deja de echar arena!

💋 dayha day echar arayna

Mind my eyes!

¡Cuidado con mis ojos!

💋 kweedado kon mees ohos

sandcastle
el castillo de arena
👄 el casteeyo day arayna

sea
el mar
👄 el mar

beach la playa
👄 la playa

towel
la toalla
👄 la toe-aya

swimming costume
el bañador
👄 el banyador

bucket el cubo
👄 el koobo

snorkel
el tubo
👄 el toobo

shells
las conchas
👄 las konchas

spade
la pala
👄 la palla

It's going swimmingly!

How to make a splash in Spanish!

PLOF

Let's hit the swimming pool
Vamos a la piscina

🗣 bamos a la peeseena

Can you swim (underwater)?
¿Sabes nadar (debejo del agua)? 🗣 sabays nedar (debaho del agwa)

Me too/I can't
Yo también/Yo no

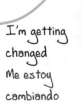

🗣 yo tambeeyen/ yo no

I'm getting changed
Me estoy cambiando

🗣 may estoy kambee-ando

Can you dive?
¿Te sabes tirar de cabeza?

🗣 tay sabays teerar day kabaytha

Can you swim ...?
¿Sabes nadar ...?

💬 sabays nadar

... backstroke
a espalda

💬 a espalda

... butterfly
a mariposa

💬 a mareeposa

... crawl
a crol

💬 a krol

... breaststroke
a braza 💬 a bratha

slide
el tobogán

💬 el tobogan

goggles
las gafas

💬 las gafas

77

Downtown

Pooper-scoopers on wheels

You might see bright green-and-white motorcycles with funny vacuum cleaners on the side riding around town scooping up the dog poop. The people riding the bikes look like astronauts! (Well, you'd want protection too, wouldn't you?)

Do you know the way?
¿Te sabes el camino?
🗣 tay sabays el kameeno

Let's ask
Vamos a preguntar
🗣 bamos a pray-
goontar

bus
el autobús
🗣 el owtoboos

Is it far?

¿Está lejos?

🫦 esta lay-hos

Are we allowed in here?

¿Nos dejan entrar aquí?

🫦 nos day-han entrar akee

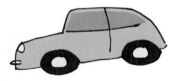

car

el coche

🫦 el kochay

You could gain a lot of street cred with your new Spanish friends by using a bit of slang.
A clapped-out car is *"una cafetera"* (*oona cafaytayra*), which means "coffee pot"! Try this: *"¡Vaya cafetera!"* (*baya cafaytayra* – "What an old banger!").

Park yourself here

swings los columpios
👄 los koloom-peeyos

climbing frame el juego para escalar 👄 el hway-go para eska-lar

playground el patio de recreo
👄 el pateeyo day rekrayo

grass la hierba
👄 la yairba

tree el árbol
👄 el ar-bol

slide
el tobogán
👄 el tobogan

park el parque 👄 el parkay

Can we play ball games?

¿Podemos jugar a la pelota?

🗨 poday-mos hoo-gar a la pay-lota

roundabout

el tiovivo

🗨 el tio-beebo

sandpit

el arenero

🗨 el arain-airo

Can I have a go? ¿Puedo intentarlo?

🗨 pwaydo intain-tarloe

81

Picnics

I hate wasps

Odio las avispas

🗣 odeeyo las abeespas

Move over!

¡Apártate!

🗣 apar-tatay

Shall we sit here?

¿Nos sentamos aquí?

🗣 nos sentamos akee

bread

el pan 🗣 el pan

napkin

la servilleta

🗣 la serbeeyeta

ham el jamón

🗣 el hamon

cheese

el queso

🗣 el kayso

yoghurt

el yogurt

🗣 el yogurt

crisps

las patatas fritas

🗣 las patatas freetas

drinks

las bebidas

👄 las bebeedas

knife

el cuchillo

👄 el koocheeyo

spoon

la cuchara

👄 la koochara

fork

el tenedor

👄 el tenaydor

wasps

las avispas

👄 las abeespas

bees

las abejas

👄 las abayhas

bzzzz

ants

las hormigas

👄 las ormeegas

Wake up, campers!

tent la tienda
🔊 la tyen-da

tent peg
la piqueta
🔊 la pee-kayta

camper van
la caravana
🔊 la kara-vana

penknife
la navaja de bolsillo
🔊 la nava-ha day bol-seelyo

camping stove
el camping gas
🔊 el "camping gas"

sleeping bag el saco de dormir
🔊 el sak-ko day door-meer

torch la linterna
🔊 la lin-air-na

That tent's a palace!
Jo, ¡vaya tienda!
👄 ho, buy-ya tyen-da

Is there a campfire?
¿Hay una hoguera?
👄 ay oona og-waira

I've lost my torch
He perdido mi linterna
👄 eh pairdeedo mee lintair-na

These showers are gross!
¡Las duchas están sucias!
👄 las doo-chas estan soothyas

Where does the rubbish go?
¿Dónde se tira la basura?
👄 donday say teera la bascoora

85

All the fun of the fair

helter-skelter
el tobogán
 el tobogan

big wheel
la noria
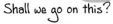 la noreeya

house of mirrors
la casa de los espejos
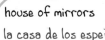 la kasa day los espayhos

bumper cars
los coches de choque
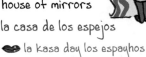 los kochays
day chokay

Shall we go on this?
¿Nos montamos en éste?
nos montamos en estay

86

roundabout

el pulpo

💋 el poolpo

That's for babies

Eso es para los pequeños

💋 eso es para los pekay-nyos

It's very fast

Va muy rápido

💋 ba mwee rapeedo

Do you get wet in here?

¿En éste te mojas?

💋 en estay tay mohas

I'm not going on my own

Yo solo no me monto

💋 yo solo no may monto

Disco nights

mirror ball
la bola de espejos
 la bola day espay-hos

loudspeaker
el altavoz
 el altab-oth

Can I request a song?
¿Puedo pedir una canción?
 pwaydo paydeer oona kan-thyon

The music is really lame
¡La música es malísima!
 la mooseeka es malee-seema

spotlights
los focos
 los fo-kos

DJ
el pinchadiscos
 el peencha-deeskos

turntable
el tocadiscos
 el toka-deeskos

How old do I need to be?

¿Cuántos años hay que tener?

🗨 kwantos anyos ay kay tenair

dance floor

la pista de baile

🗨 la peesta day balay

Let's dance!

¡Vamos a bailar!

🗨 ba-mos a balar

I love this song!

¡Me encanta esta canción!

🗨 may enkanta esta kan-thyon

89

POCKET MONEY

sweets
los caramelos
👄 los karamaylos

T-shirts
las camisetas
👄 las kameesetas

toys
los juguetes
👄 los hoogetes

el tendero
👄 el tendayro

books

los libros

 los leebros

el móvil

🗨 el mobeel

pencils

los lápices

🗨 los lapeethes

POCKET MONEY

What does that sign say?

Carnicería

butcher shop
carnicería
🗣 karneethereeya

cake shop
pastelería
🗣 pasteler
—reeya

Pastelería

bakery
panadería
🗣 panadereeya

Panadería

sweet shop
confitería
🗣 confeeter-reeya

Verdulería

stationers
papelería
🗣 papelereeya

PAPELERÍA

greengrocer
verdulería
🗣 berdooler-reeya

clothes shop
boutique
🗣 booteek

Boutique

Do you have some cash?

¿Tienes pasta?

💋 tee-enes pasta

I'm broke

No tengo un duro

💋 no tengo oon dooro

I'm loaded

Estoy forrado

💋 estoy forrado

Here you go

Aquí tienes

💋 akee tee-enes

That's a weird shop!

¡Vaya tienda más rara!

💋 buy-ya tyen-da mas ra-ra

That's a bargain Eso es una ganga

💋 eso es oona ganga

It's a rip-off

Es un robo

💋 es oon robo

93

Sweet heaven!

I love this shop

Me encanta esta tienda

 💬 may enkanta esta tee-enda

Let's get some sweets

Vamos a comprar chucherías

💬 bamos a comprar choochereeyas

Let's get some ice cream

Vamos por un helado

💬 bamos por oon aylado

lollipops

las piruletas

💬 las peerooletas

a bar of chocolate

una tableta de chocolate

💬 oona tableta day chokolatay

chewing gum

el chicle

💬 el cheeklay

94

If you really want to look Spanish and end up with lots of fillings, ask for:

regaliz

(regaleez)
soft licorice sticks, available in red or black

polvos pica-pica

(polvos peeka peeka)
tangy fizzy sherbet sold in small packets with a lollipop to dip in

jamones
(hamon-nes)
fruity, fizzy gums in the shape of hams ("ham" is **jamón**)

Chupa-chups®

(choopa-choops)
lollies famous all over the world, but they come from Spain

nubes (noobes)
soft marshmallow sweets ("flumps") in different shades (**nubes** means clouds)

 kilométrico
(keelomay-treeko)
chewing gum in a strip like dental floss – pretend to the adults that you're flossing your teeth!

95

Other things you could buy
(that won't ruin your teeth!)

What are you getting?

¿Qué te vas a comprar?

👄 kay tay bas a komprar

That toy, please

Ese juguete, por favor

👄 esay hoogetay, por fabor

Two postcards, please

Dos postales, por favor

👄 dos postal-les, por fabor

This is rubbish

Esto es una porquería

👄 esto es oona porkayreeya

This is cool

Esto mola

👄 esto mola

I'm
getting ...
Voy a
comprar
👄 bcy a
comprar

... a pen
... un boli
👄 oon bolee

... stamps
... sellos
👄 seyos

... felt-tip pens
... rotuladores
👄 rotoolador-res

Lápices de Colores

... coloured pencils
... lápices de colores
👄 lapeethes day kolor-res

... a key ring
... un llavero
👄 oon
yabairo

... comics
... tebeos
👄 taybayos

97

... a fridge magnet

... un imán de nevera

🗨 oon ee-man day

nay-baira

... a shell box

... un joyero de conchas

🗨 oon ho-yairo day

konchas

... a necklace

un collar

🗨 oon koyar

How much is that?

¿Cuánto cuesta?

🗨 kwanto kwesta

For many years Spain's favourite comics have been *Mortadelo y Filemón*, two accident-prone TIA agents (<u>not</u> CIA) and *Zipi y Zape*, two very naughty twins. Children also like to read *Mafalda*, an Argentinian comic, *Carlitos y Snoopy* (Charlie Brown & Snoopy), Tintin, Astérix and *¿Dónde está Wally?* (Where's Wally?).

Money talks

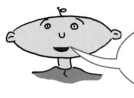

How much pocket money do you get?

¿Cuánto te dan de paga?

🫘 kwanto tay dan day pa-ga

I only have this much

Sólo tengo esto

🫘 soul-lo tain-go esto

Can you lend me ten euros?

¿Me prestas diez euros?

🫘 may praystas deeyeth ay-ooros

No way!

¡Ni hablar!

🫘 nee ablar

Spanish money is the **euro** (pronounced *ay-ooro*).
A euro is divided into 100 **centimos** (*thainteemos*).
Coins: 1, 2, 5, 10, 20, 50 **centimos**
       1, 2 **euros**
Notes: 5, 10, 20, 50, 100 **euros**
Make sure you know how much you are spending before you blow all your pocket money at once!

GROWN UP TALK

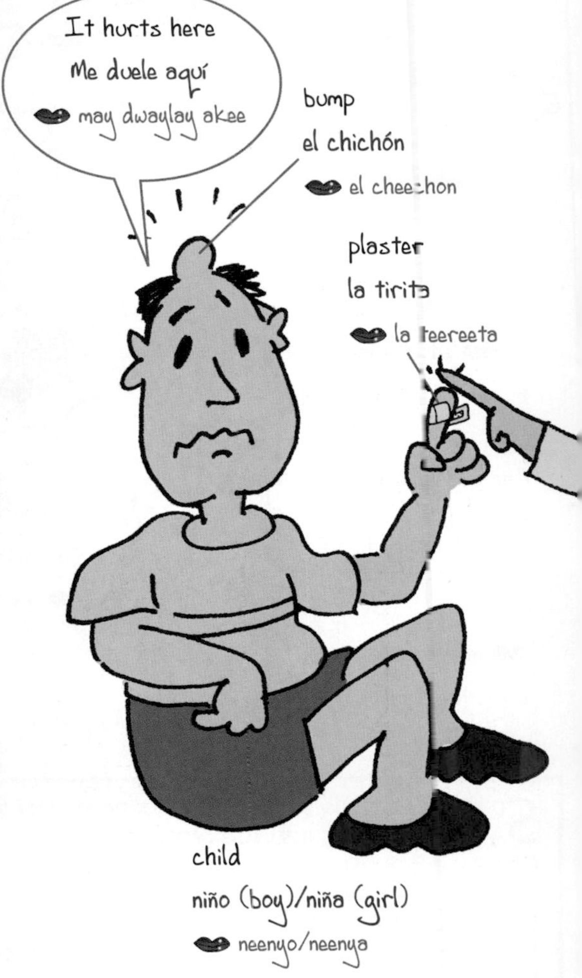

Help!

Something has dropped/broken
Algo se ha caído/roto

💋 algo say a kigh-eedo/roto

Please
Por favor

💋 por fabor

Can you help me?
¿Me puedes ayudar?

💋 may pwedes ayoodar

Where's the post box?
¿Dónde está el buzón?

💋 donday esta el boothon

Where are the toilets?
¿Dónde están los aseos?

💋 donday estan los asayos

I can't manage it

No puedo

🗣 no pwedo

Could you pass me that?

¿Me pasas eso?

🗣 may pasas eso

What time is it?

¿Qué hora es?

🗣 kay ora es

Come and see

Ven a ver

🗣 ben a bair

May I look at your watch?

¿Me deja que mire su reloj?

🗣 may deha kay meera soo reloh

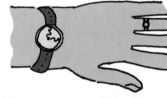

103

Lost for words

I've lost ...
He perdido ...
👄 eh perdeedo

... my ticket
mi billete

👄 mee beeyaytay

... my mobile
mi móvil

👄 mee mo-beel

... my parents
mis padres

👄 mees padrays

104

... my shoes
mis zapatos

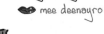 mees thapatos

... my money mi dinero

 mee deenayro

... my jumper
mi jersey

 mee hersay

... my watch
mi reloj

 mee reloh

... my jacket mi chaqueta

 mee chakayta

105

Adults only!

Show this page to adults who can't seem to make themselves clear (it happens). They will point to a phrase, you read what they mean, and you should all understand each other perfectly.

No te preocupes
Don't worry

Siéntate aquí
Sit down here

¿Tu nombre y apellidos?
What's your name and surname?

¿Cuántos años tienes?
How old are you?

¿De dónde eres?
Where are you from?

¿Dónde te alojas?
Where are you staying?

¿Dónde te duele?
Where does it hurt?

¿Eres alérgico a algo?
Are you allergic to anything?

Está prohibido
It's forbidden

Tiene que acompañarte un adulto
You have to have an adult with you

Voy por alguien que hable inglés
I'll get someone who speaks English

EXTRA STUFF

weather
el tiempo
el tyem-po

numbers los números los noo-mairos

1

3

time

la hora

la ora

EXTRA STUFF

Numbers

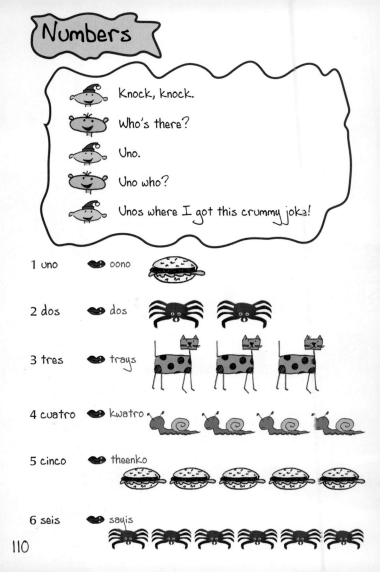

Knock, knock.

Who's there?

Uno.

Uno who?

Unos where I got this crummy joke!

1 uno — oono

2 dos — dos

3 tres — trays

4 cuatro — kwatro

5 cinco — theenko

6 seis — sayis

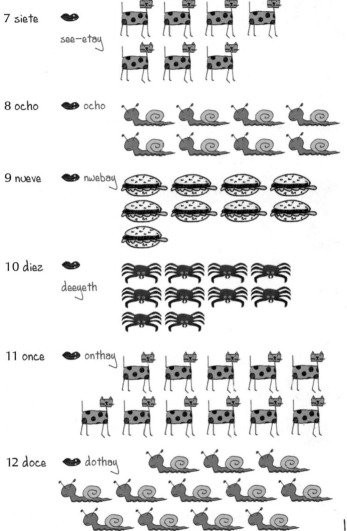

7 siete · see-etay

8 ocho · ocho

9 nueve · nwebay

10 diez · deeyeth

11 once · onthay

12 doce · dothay

trece  trethay

catorce 👄 katorthay

quince 👄 keenthay

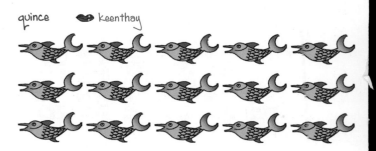

16	dieciséis	*deeyethee sayis*
17	diecisiete	*deeyethee see-etay*
18	dieciocho	*deeyethee ocho*
19	diecinueve	*ceeyethee nwebay*

If you want to say "thirty-two", "fifty-four" and so on, you can just put the two numbers together like you do in English. But don't forget to add the word for "and" (**y** – *ee*) in the middle:

32	treinta y dos	*traynta ee dos*
54	cincuenta y cuatro	*theenkwenta ee kwatro*
81	ochenta y uno	*ochenta ee oono*

20	viente	*baintay*
30	treinta	*traynta*
40	cuarenta	*kwarenta*
50	cincuenta	*theenkwenta*
60	sesenta	*saysenta*
70	setenta	*saytenta*
80	ochenta	*ochenta*
90	noventa	*nobenta*
100	cien	*theeyen*

a thousand mil *meel*

a million un millón *oon meel-yon*

a gazillion! tropecientos! *tropay- theeyentos*

114

1st	primero	*preemairo*
2nd	segundo	*segoondo*
3rd	tercero	*terthayro*
4th	cuarto	*kwarto*
5th	quinto	*keento*
6th	sexto	*sexto*
7th	séptimo	*septeemo*
8th	octavo	*octabo*
9th	noveno	*nobayno*
10th	décimo	*daytheemo*

Fancy a date?

If you want to say a date in Spanish, you don't need to use 1st, 2nd, etc. Just say the ordinary number followed by *de* (*day*):

Lunes	Martes	Miércoles	Jueves	Viernes	Sábado	Domingo
		1	2	3	4	5
6	7	8	9	10	11	12
13	14	15	16	17	18	19
20	21	22	23	24	25	26
27	28	29	30			

uno de marzo   (1st of March)

diez de julio   (10th of July)

Months

March	marzo	*martho*
April	abril	*abreel*
May	mayo	*my-yo*

June	junio	*hooneeyo*
July	julio	*hooleeyo*
August	agosto	*agosto*

September	septiembre	*septee-embray*
October	octubre	*octoobray*
November	noviembre	*nobee-embray*

December	diciembre	*deethee-embray*
January	enero	*enayro*
February	febrero	*febrayro*

Seasons

primavera *preemabayra*

verano *berano*

otoño *otonyo*

invierno *eenbee-erno*

Days of the week

Monday	lunes	*loon-nes*
Tuesday	martes	*mar-tes*
Wednesday	miércoles	*mee-erkol-les*
Thursday	jueves	*hoo-ebes*
Friday	viernes	*bee-er-nes*
Saturday	sábado	*sabado*
Sunday	domingo	*domeengo*

By the way, Spanish kids have a two-and-a-half hour lunch break! Time enough for lunch and a siesta. But they don't finish until 5pm in the afternoon.

Good times

It's ...
Son ...
👄 sonn

(five) o'clock
las (cinco)
👄 las (theenko)

quarter past (two)
las (dos) y cuarto
👄 las (dos) ee kwar-o

quarter to (four)
las (cuatro) menos cuarto
👄 las (kwatro) menos kwarto

half past (three)
las (tres) y media
👄 las (trays) ee media

five past (ten)

las (diez) y cinco

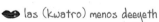 las (deeyeth) ee theenko

twenty past (eleven)

las (once) y viente

las (onthay) ee baintay

ten to (four)

las (cuatro) menos diez

las (kwatro) menos deeyeth

twenty to (six)

las (seis) menos veinte

las (sayis) menos baintay

Watch out for "one o'clock". It's a bit different from the other times. If you want to say "It's one o'clock" you have to say **Es la una** (*es la oona*). "It's half past one" is **Es la una y media** (*es la oona ee medya*), and so on.

morning

mañana

 la manyarna

midday
mediodía

el medyo-deeya

afternoon

la tarde

la tarday

midnight
la medianoche

la medya-nochay

evening la noche

la nochay

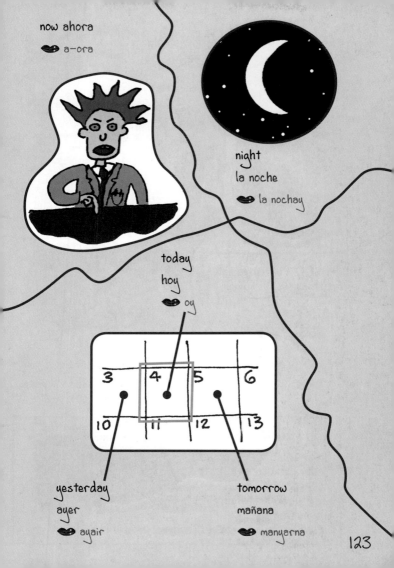

123

Weather wise

Can we go out?

¿Podemos salir fuera?

💋 podaymos saleer fwera

It's hot

Hace calor

💋 athay kalor

It's cold

Hace frío

💋 athay freeyo

It's horrible

Hace un día horritle

💋 athay oon deeya orreeblay

It's raining seas!

In Spanish it doesn't rain "cats and dogs", it rains "seas"! That's what they say when it's raining really heavily:

¡Está lloviendo a mares! *esta yobeeyendo a mar-res*

It's windy

Hace viento

👄 athay beeyento

It's sunny

Hace sol

👄 athay sol

It's raining

Está lloviendo

👄 esta yobeeyendo

It's snowing

Está nevando

👄 esta nebando

I'm soaked

Estoy empapado

👄 estoy empapardo

It's nice Hace bueno

👄 athay bweno

Signs of life

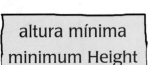

altura mínima

minimum Height

Móviles
prohibidos

No mobiles

Entrada prohibida

No entry

Sólo mayores
de 18

Over 18s only

Sólo menores de 5
Under 5s only

NO FUNCIONA

OUT OF ORDER

PRIVATE

Privado

Caballeros

Señoras